CIRCA

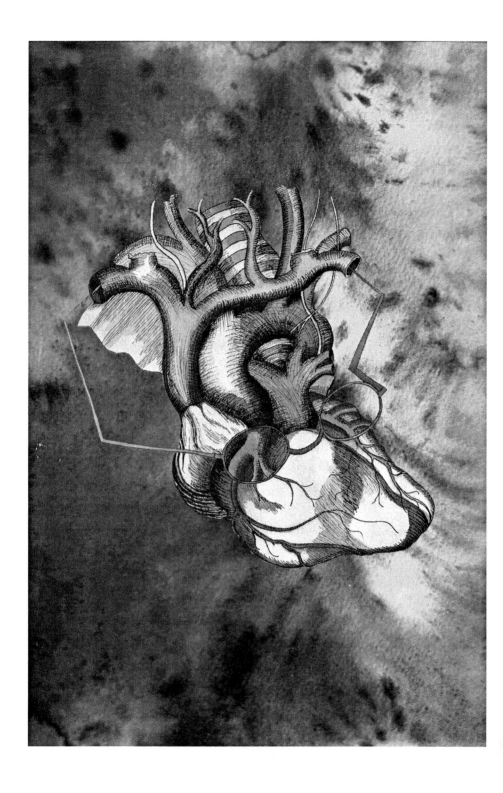

CIRCA

Hannah Zeavin

Hanging Loose Press
Brooklyn, New York
and
The Scholastic Art & Writing Awards

Published by Hanging Loose Press, 231 Wyckoff Street, Brooklyn, New York 11217. All Rights Reserved. No part of this book may be reproduced without the publisher's written permission, except for brief quotations in reviews.

www.hangingloosepress.com

Printed in the United States of America
10 9 8 7 6 5 4 3 2 1

Hanging Loose thanks the Literature Program of the New York State Council on the Arts for a grant in support of the publication of this book.

Art by Zoë Lescaze

This book is published in association with the Alliance for Young Artists & Writers, Inc., part of the Scholastic Art & Writing Awards.

Library of Congress Cataloging-in-Publication Data

Zeavin, Hannah.
  Circa / Hannah Zeavin.
    p. cm.
  Poems.
  ISBN 978-1-934909-09-6
  I. Title
  PS3626.E22C57 2009
  811'.6--dc22
                           2008046780

Produced at The Print Center, Inc. 225 Varick St., New York, NY 10014, a non-profit facility for literary and arts-related publications. (212) 206-8465

Contents

For Marty

I Once Looked at a Tapestry and Unmade It like a Monk

I rose up this morning with sickness
on my face, feeling it out with my hand

I hit myself over my head
and floated out to sea
that is when I claimed escape
as he claimed escape:

> no more no good
> his crew has died
> thank you for three-headed
> creatures on every island
> nothing but dumb
> distraction from this mast
> when the last map
> has fallen from beside my body
> into the ebb
> then shall I be carried

So went to wash and waited to go under
to the bottom of the basin and away
to an impossible corner where wheat
has never risen:

> between my toes horrible silt
> shaded ever by women with hands
> full of wild palms and folded lips
> and scaled legs and yellow tongues
> and broken eyes
> skulls alive after
> being buried in the sand
> talking spears and bile into the mouths

of young girls and then fell
asleep there, turning about one,
around, and woke up
gray where once was heather

How quiet I could walk on high to you
no one aware when the line was cut
only noticed when the missing axe appeared
to them on the wrong side of the ocean:

        weeks and weeks to get back to you
        love living below the palace
        thousands of trumpeters thundering
        shrill for any number of false returns
        and there I was, winding further
        in the wind.
        Years—bound she was
        when I appeared.
        Threads in her hair and on every wrist
        bone, nail, tooth
        from every bone, nail, and tooth
        when I came back to dine at my table
        and when I came home, I had to wash
        my feet to be received at my table
        had to scrape this sickness
        rid my lungs of this water, this ocean
        sitting there in the middle of my belly
        old, and bloated anyway, no longer
        looking the prince from any kind of sane
        province

It would have been better to die before
beginning away:

knelt no more, my love she straightens
and comes to the table and tells me no bed
but ours has been taken, she sees that
my bed has been a cave, it reads so
no more is each knot to be cut and unwound
to make the calendar, to locate the day.

Our New House

The Fates, the Graces & I took a walk up the mountain to sit, backs aligned in a row against a ruin of a church. This was our first home together, our new house, & evenings were spent pulling the shades down, so that men off the roads would not stop to ask for bed & rosemary liquor. The Fates braided one another's hair in a circle while cutting apron strings and fishing line. 1, 2, 3, 7 inches. The Graces bathed in a deep bath abandoned by the Romans, who hiked this way the year before we settled ourselves, with our kitchen and our noise.

I am not so happy here. I was never given a sister and so when the ghosts of the Muses come, though I hate them, they pretend to live, and I pretend they are mine.

Two Farm Hands to Make a Point

In the corner we think on "When"
remarking on thousands of screaming heretics in the pale morning
greeting hell fire through fire
we think on those going down to the river
meeting salvation in the flaccid water

We resolve
season turns from those in the river
to those in the heat
around the corner
from the flayed heretics all are stripping down
to their selfish bloomers
the pleats around their waists
more charming than the bleating that streams from the aether

We sit there
not looking at each other
just onto the startled faces
our minds working over "It must"
for all is staked on being rejoined

We will go down
before Moses and sit on the boat
place coins from coupled hands
over eyelids, stay our breath
see which river, where it bends.

Boy/Girl

Skull amphibian, thighs visible,
30,000 bones 30,000 leagues down
the girl late to expose
Mama told me I was once a whale

My father said I was the greatest
disappointment since D-Day
broken and blistered and splintered bodies
and I could think: bodies of armor

Only in death do we look the mammal
skull amphibian, thighs visible
where flora sit in the dark
the girl late to expose

I sipped heavy water to try and not
my father said I was the greatest
I sipped to not hear him
broken and blistered and splintered bodies

Sitting under a wood slab at night
only in death do we look the mammal
best learn what it feels like
where flora sit in the dark

I once fell asleep next to mine
I sipped heavy water to try and not
listen to his rib cage breathe so
I sipped to not hear him

And mothers look the father
sitting under a wood slab at night

big bodies moving through big bodies
best learn what it feels like

We were brothers but I was the sister
I once fell asleep next to mine
and then gave him over to the baby
listen to his rib cage breathe so

If I were my brother and he were me
and mothers look the father
I would be the size of a grapefruit
big bodies moving through big bodies

I was D-Day and he?
we were brothers but I was the sister
and I took this leech and they said don't
and then gave him over to the baby

I could find a man the size of a minnow
if I were my brother and he were me
we would be cleaved: a grapefruit and
I would be the size of a grapefruit.

Father looked at me once more to think greatest
disappointment since D-Day
my father died that morning, now my son
and I could think: bodies of armor

Structures and structures of ourselves,
30,000 bones 30,000 leagues down
charted forever on boats above.
Mama told me I was once a whale.

When the Sun Came Up and You Were Bent

Grandmaster, where is your horse?
Where is the sun to stain each
winded blown brow?

Where are your sons, each
William
Where is your continental
overlap, as in Texas
that glacial Venn diagram?

Where does your compass point?
True north: west.
Magnetic forces
do shift with the will of Destiny.
(Ford one more hill, dawn.
One more river. The sea.)

Farmer replaces farmer, with
mule and bullet. Horse hand
takes horse, then passes from
hand to hand—

How to continue the odyssey?
You've greeted your sailors
at the breast, bit each
bare nape of the neck.

You've lost them, each
crowing these seven years
in dire straits.

What comment on the maelstrom
that interrupted the shirtless, shanghaied
return?

Grandmaster, have you a word to say?
Your amplification fixed, your drink poured.

Where can I find it?
Between which gilded shelves can I listen?
Where will I find your cleaved idol?

Where Man Is in His Whole

The heart on the breast of my mother
Saint, sleeping on the wing
of any number of blackbirds
their feet sticking out the end
of red pies.

Danger is my jester,
is the only thing keeping me here.

He holds nothing to himself.
In public he goes public.

There is a man who takes
blue silt to his brow
and kisses pollen.

No one notices.

They call him their leader.

Between breast in the morning
and open arms at night

Clouds of hair:
Gin guard has toes splayed to
receive me to receive me.

Songs and clouds and
pots banged. It's natural,
it's considered natural here.

In the Hollars

The Great White Hope
sealed the windows
and blanched my eye
and so set out
across leagues of rivers
and plains and came
around onto a bend:

Three hundred people

Two attached to wooden
signs, feet signaling
direction by their
painted toes

Logs linger in the bays,
bathing like bleating whales
breeching in the wind, tide
so I turned these into jibless boats
and with no sail my fleet bore no seal,
carried forth no cargo
passed through no borders of several nations

Barley, clay, four silver bells, broken spines of crooked volumes
stuck under the seat

200 settlements like this:

All bare-legged
6,000 humans running

None have yet discovered
the violin of wood and bone
have not chalked the hair
from horses' tails as it gathers
in the rush and bramble—

Just hundreds of uses for skin and feather

They truly are akin to thieves of fire.

All My Friends

The oblong-framed Victorian peeled her socks down
her legs and exposed her
ankles

I looked

She turned around and while kicking up her heels
she yelled at me to
turn around to
stop looking

Her eyes were the color of the best of sauces
and her ankles themselves akin to cows

She covered the legs of her tables but not her own

> Perfectly invasive, perfectly invasive,
> you are a cannibal, a cannibal, you are
> a barbarian, you are
>
> You knew I was hungry and you said that you'd rather watch
> the buzzards and the beasties of prey
> watch the beasts of prey get to work.

This Is What You

This was once where I went: the hills of Mexico
High with tales to tell, we walked forward, eating
Only what was out of fields. We knew where
We were by night, lying down, hearing 300 banks
Of rivers somewhere, an odd pair of kin kissing.
You and I carried one case and one cloak and wrapped
Ourselves in a sailor's sail when it became light where
We couldn't see over—
We had a drum and a telephone, no dial,
So we wandered into a village and married and died.

This was once what I found, lying
Down, wishing for a statue at breach to my breast:
Knowing what's mine, what with this body here,
Mine or yours no matter— Folly like 600 sculpted
English gardens. Solemnly saluting in the sun, sand
Slandering our noses, no artists to render us slender.
It is wicked to be made animated and not to speak.
Sitting here, garden at one and house at the other,
Both sadly unbearable, retained like me, no reason:
My fault for not kissing the girl with snakes like a rosary.

This is what once was said: the best feature
Is the clementine you hold, your legs have nothing
But a sense of humor to recommend them,
You did not think out the tableaux you are: too busy
With what is beneath your feet—rocks,
Dinosaurs dissolved, the fabric spitting—
I wish it were possible that you in
Your blue legs and me in my yellow coat could always
Think upon moments and carpets, plain as day and day goes.
I did not reply, no speech granted, I sat and looked at the granite.

This was once true: I had never loved and was fatigued.
Then, three: Pied Piper, Peter Pan, C.K. Dexter Haven, myself, the party
Of four set out every morning, set to exercise, talking relief
Into a napkin square, taking small muffins, glass bottle brought to collect milk.
Sometimes, we would meet the Lecturer, kiss his dog
Between collar and bone as he ran down
The lane. Sometimes, when invited up, retiring from the summer,
We would knock heads opening doors, all in browns we would set up a
Magic lantern in the living room. The Lecturer, coughing, would advance
Slides of the countryside as the early setting sun caught the white of
Skeleton ribs leaning against windows: enamel on enamel. Out of boxes, they,
      on holiday.

The Song of Nick Dodge Eating Marissa Perel

I saw the bird explode overhead
feathers falling little gnats of blood
and your shotgun dropped to my foot:
you call this dinner.

Somewhere around a campfire later,
set under a rock we decided that sleep

would lead to three hundred bears
and one or two foxes. Our bird
hung high anyway, and kept us looking
for it, wanting another, or an oxen.

The morning came and I got up,
lay woodslats at your feet to box
you in and took that shotgun to your feet.

I couldn't know that hunger would be
so, here, in our party,
15,000 feet up, at this overpass.

You woke up with a shudder and sneeze
and watched me clip a round, two.

Fox Molder & Dana Scully came to look for you,
could not find, not until opening my stomach cavity
did they realize that your arm said Rise as
the juices bid it hide.

Waiting on the Gesture

The Good Gesture Idiot
works in the dumb show—

The good Jester
works through the dumb show,
horrible silence,
chalk—

The Good Gesture Idiot,
covered in terrible silence,
white paint, cream,
sliding on sweat—

Tracks around the eye,
aqueduct delivery—

Lines the tracks around the eye
tear duct delivery—

Lifts the glass to wooden
lips, curtain parts

Lifts the glass to swollen lips,
curtain opens on Man and Idiot,
no reverse end of the telescope
for the sympathetic audience—

This systematic Gesture,
this symptomatic Jester,
he does not dare break it now,
no, the Gesture won't end now.

In front of the mirror with scissors
and a comb—

Over the stage door,
out the window with a glass of sherry—

On the steps of the stage
over a bucket, cutting loose
locks from his bloated
hair-stache

The Jester takes the Patron by the hand,
the Gesture by the other—

Takes one meat hand in one
lily hand, the wooden
hand in two, turns for the couch—

In the drawing room the Jester
draws up the Patron's skirts, she writes
up a check—

Face down, the Jester
is on the Lady's neck,
The Good Gesture Idiot
plays two nights weekly
in the dumb show, he sits
on the shelf—

The Jester is starving, is starting
to sweat off his spread: sprayed
cotton wig, leather shoes,
silver tie, suspenders—

In the mirror, the Patron
catches with scissors
and a comb the loose
lint from between limber
fingers—

The Jester drinks Kahlúa
in the kitchen. He undoes
the Patron, the Good Gesture
Idiot kisses the clock,
he is not embarrassed—

The Good Gesture Idiot
is not embarrassed to hear
the Jester giggling, no,
the Patron giggling,
the Jester groveling,
their lily hands groping—

The Girl, the goat,
the Jester, ahead,
gaming with piano player's
hands covering Opera
Lady's bosom—
The Jester sneaks off silver rings
and damns the Patron,
dancing around her back—

In public he goes in public,
the Patron is private about
how she spends her money
in public—

Piano player's hands
around a wasted waist,
with worried posture,
a worked play—

The Patron's knees
are released,
let go of their squeeze, spasm,
and the Jester notices the gesture—

The Jester has her purse
now, he knows, and takes
her along with it—

The Jester, Good Gesture
Idiot thrown over his arm,
takes his solid coat off the hook
and casts it over soiled pants—

The Jester works in the dumb show.
The Good Gesture Idiot works through the dumb show,
horrible silence, sliding paint, sweat silence in front of a mirror
he mimes it back at the Jester with scissors and a comb—

The Good Gesture Idiot sits on a stool on stage
slouching, stooped shoulders, no telescope
on the symptomatic audience for the sly manic
Jester—

No, it does not get broken,
no, it was in the drawing
room, not over the stage door
drinking a glass of sherry,
not drinking a glass of sherry
over the sink—

No, it was drinking a glass
of bourbon in the boudoir,
lifting the glass to wooden lips,
he lifts the glass to swollen lips,
the curtain parts—

In Public

On the south shore, they laid us out in twos and threes
the fair attracted the ordinary
blue mounds took clear wheat
rush and thistle guiding stems of stalks in.

The staff and plaster on the altar and then
here we go, watching it cement
in the morning
the first after the last of us crowded in.

There will be 16,000 light bulbs
where there are towers. You will see new
and do not be blinded where they fall.
Wretched they will feel, jarring your shadow
from your back, flaming your outline
making you thin.

The city is fleeing the earth on our back
alabaster now riddled, now heather, turning grey
a mother whispers in.

Listens in, the boats on the water, they all came here,
it was so long before you, it made you, you could not speak it.
It carried the firsts, the fists of the Furies,
but not the first of disease here. That spread
out, like our great fire, but it did not end them
like the fire did not end me.

The peaks are everywhere when you walk down the lane
you will get lost, and so, take a quarter. We will meet at
a show, if separated.

If you must sup, sit alone at a table, you must
one day you will know what this feels like
but let me better you now by scything it for you
saving the end years for the end.

You may be riddled, sitting on a platform
watching 300 specimens on a bank, reaching
forward, prisoners touching fingertips through the partition.
On the south shore, you can watch them marching
playing the visitor, they have lists dangling from their fingers.

Wives with their husbands marching, perhaps their brothers
sit in the granite railway. They are as if in a tank
sweating in their hats, the brow bands sinking
into shades of tobacco stains, loose dirt
slumping down, darkening their brows.

Others sit on the switch, accidentally convoluting
the sideswipe of swinging cars.

If you lose my hand, if you get loose
by the water, look for the boats and call out loud

If you get lost, if I lose you, we will find each other
down by the sanded water, where nothing has risen,
where they direct us to pass directly.

Along the tracks, some ship home their purchases
from City Beautiful, a postcard sent ahead to predict
date of arrival. They sell the cookstove
so as to steal off the south shore, moving
off of the brief podiums littering the streets, and the stands
unwinding to welcome them.

There is no natural here; you cannot find it out
sitting above, below any number of others

Turn again, and you will be back by the water
on the long, listless walk

Pillowcases line every off avenue, do not use
them as markers. They are in the business
of airing out nights of complaints
and to them, you are nothing but a circulating
breeze, sent to circumvent the weather.

The Last Normal Visitor

I was born on the Charles River, Mexico
My tongue learned to spell out trespasses
So I could tell all the mermaid babies the quatrains
Of their fathers, ghosts of pirate people
As taught to me when they still had their taut cheeks.

This was your year, so long back:
These total secrets seemed nothing
But local songs to sequester into their children's
Ear by the long shore, where the beach ran
Beyond and the Ferris wheel was turned off
So that there were no lights but the night
Fishermen and the cars coming to pick up
The passengers getting off the first ferry.

My first friend had no hearing in her left head,
her right held little. When I sang
Her the song of her father, chopping
Humiliated heifers & hundreds of schools
Of fish on the docks, we kissed.

In the garden out back we wandered a tangle
And romped a while and spotted a rabbit.
We held hostage and for ransom the potted plum
Pie her mother made for the weekend holiday.

I was made out of *my* mother's apron
Strings, and our relations grew
In the bedroom over blocks and cards
From Grandpa in Japan. No one could
Have noticed that we weren't eating oysters
As we were always told to do, for our
Brothers were always ready and willing
To lie on our feet, under the table.

We Were Married in 1920

It was underneath horsefeet
with babes in knees
and knees to chest:
and lips to elbow:
that we first,

And second—
we succumbed to the red
we lay, lay in fields of wheat
shivering in open sun, looking
for the warm back of a tree
we never found

Bible in witch county

We kept looking
and also found a fish,
Devil, in a cranberry pond
and filleted in

Fingers living in pie
so we sipped Devil down/out
of her skull. No fork.
And it was when we were married
"if fact" before you were born.

Diva Dolorosa, Hallucinating in Her Closet

Lady has escaped to her wardrobe
noon wedding an hour behind;
bends beckoning; holds the hilt of a far-reaching dagger

In the corner two retching women

Doctor is called and misses his cue;
enters late; the scene a husband pacing
six hours in the corridor

The pair meet; burst into the chamber
Doctor's hands over every mouth
through every white cloth; turns to turn on
the hanging halogen light

Pomade under ever long nails;
under Doctor's orders: Lady
to lie in bed

Husband to the bed; kneels;
sticks wrist under his wife's nose;
feels the air stir on skin:
thinks her limp with love

One day, Father and Mother and Lady
on the river. The barge stops:
Mother takes her hands to her eyes, palms turn out

Lady ordered to count back from ten; eyes open;
the count finishes and Doctor and Husband
sleeping over the writing table; hands caught
in opposing jacket pockets

One day, a feather tucked between arm and breast
Lady alone at last: walks in a weeded wood, white
all the way through with broad promenade

The dairy cows and the breeding cows bellowing
into the western wind wake to begin their day
before Husband and Doctor; through the window
overlooking the pasture only they see the patient take
leave, leveraging off nightclothes and 60 lengths of loose lace

Lady in her bathroom
drops each finger's ring
ringing onto the floor; takes bottle of perfume;
slides cork out slowly; watches six drops fall to the
bottom of her pewter cup

The curtains drawn back from the bed;
Doctor panicking; a call to Saint Anthony

In the bathroom Lady turns the cup upside down;
her mouth moistens; repeats; takes bottle of perfume;
slides cork out slowly; watches six drops fall to the
bottom of her pewter cup; turns the cup upside down;
her mouth moistens

Dancing with the mirror in the garden, disarrayed in
a white dress flung open

Doctor to Husband
To the window

Husband to Doctor
See her there

Doctor to Husband
dead in the garden

Dead in the garden! "My garden, and then into the old Roman
bath, six feet deep and then the devil in me no more."
Venus' hands caught in her dress, break her roping
pearls, pull the comb from her hair.

Elephant Slaughter in an Arboretum

We were drinking coffee in teacups, placing them in the center
Of our skirts, arranging our picnic basket and cutlery
When we saw the executioner and the incandescent light bulb
On his sloped head and began to cry knowing fate to be present.

The elephant was Johnny's before a man like Barnum bought him
And brought him far from our Arboretum to the center of the city
To make him a star. The man was already a celebrity.

Johnny couldn't refuse the sum, for it meant that he could flee
The crowds that flanked our rowed houses, and he headed for Africa
To farm and find more elephants like the one he loved so dearly.

He left us in charge of making sure his elephant was fed.
We never worried until now, with the conclusion of our duties,
        our hearts heaving.
Like this we walked, my cousin and I, our fingers intertwined,
        lingering closer.

The executioner took the light bulb off his head and to the ground
        the elephant went.
The air carried no smell as it was a horrid day for boat racing to begin with.
& like they did Antigone, they forbade us to bury the monstrosity for it
        was to be, they said,
good fertilizer for the flowers we enjoyed so dearly.

The Emergence Of

Father, I learned this

The Cinderman has a close friend with a younger sister
to whom he writes letters and reworks the smudges
in the margins where his hand lingered too close
at night when the soprano shifts down to slow
and brings in the dusk
in his cylinder of wax

by the light of his own incandescence

his life becomes a series of conquerings
the bettering of parlor wit
redrawing the day into and long

Once, he twirled fingers over telegraphs
looking at shocking news of women leaving men
and of daughters searching for mothers
and of nothing of import to report:
"I cannot watch right now
the cold front lifting and other weathers
taking its place"

The man who sits
in Menlo Park on a long beached bench
leaning deeply into a wooden stretch, shaded
by his porch
peering into the shoot
the gutter to the factory
and sees neat hands
and a tired face

He thinks
if not for that wrecked brow
she could have been queen.
Is she weary?

Does she wonder about from where I draw
my patents to make our home?

It is my factory and hers.
If she is wrapping the cord of my wire
we are on a parallel circuit
start to finish we will be the start and the finish
she will keep my time and I hers
and with our simple machines and children
we will fix ourselves to the earth,
yes.

A novelty.

Nick DeBoer Is a Bank Man

Mornings, Nick kisses a blanket
on the forehead in his socks
& tucks a white shirt into white
boxers.

He does not wonder where his pants
are, nor does he check the hour
as he pours brownie batter into a pan
and places it in the oven.

After a minute with the heat on low,
he penetrates the plasma with a finger—

Not quite done, Nick thinks, Oh well.

With a spoon, ladle, and spatula, Nick
applies brownie to his kneecaps and
shoes. He puts a tie and hat on top
of his head, and without looking
at a mirror, he knows he has done well.

The bankers will love this, he remarks.

In his car, he takes care to let
his knees and shoes dry without interruption.

He thinks, today I will make millions.

Carnage

One night my father came home with his bad heart
and found his bed mussed, and me in the glare of
the refrigerator with two boys.
Both were his students.

My father had never paused while attending
to his teaching job in Cambridge: not when I was
born, not when I was almost killed, and certainly
not for any kind of awards ceremony. No, he said,
those are for people with existences that some might call paltry.

One night my father came home with his bad heart
and so when my father did not tell me who had
died, I decided it would do my father some good
if I kissed him on the forehead, crossing the floor,
smoothing my skirt and pulling my stockings
over each knee. My father then ordered me out,
and so I walked. I left the three men,
my father, the students, standing with the icebox melting.

One held my pipe. The other, my father's beer.
Between classes, I had invited them over to catch the
4 o'clock sun in the open doorway.

My father had come home with his bad heart
to dial the phone for me, order in food,
and turn to sleep. Now my father
had come home to a daughter and
his two capital scholars. We were not supposed
to be acquainted.

I feared for the two students
but then Sheila called. I took it in my room.
Sheila whispered along the line into my ear.
Marsha, she said slowly
What do you think it would be like to have a baby
in this heat?

I told her I'd think on it, but that it
was time to eat. I went downstairs.

My father had come home with his bad heart,
and made a meal for me with his frayed sleeves
up around his elbows. The meat was bleeding.

Only the outsides were cooked. It was just how
he liked it. He fancied it the right way for a man
to take his steak. And so he did. My father ate
steak only once every few months—the red meat
was lining the insides of him,
but he loved it so.

Marsha
he said with his eyes on his plate
I do forgive you, you are the innocent here, but the boys are not,
no. You will not see them again.

Three weeks later my father came home with his
bad heart in handcuffs, held by the snouts of dogs,
cornered and holed up in a chair in the kitchen,
his tenure revoked.

My lovers were gone, and so is he.
The latter lives out his sentence.
The former live on in me.

Hotel

The white is coming from the room
& each of us sits posed Roman
digesting each tongue, each movement
her hand stretches his, mine yours

& each of us sits posed Roman
& leans the length of our lean bed
her hand stretches his, mine yours,
her shirt, open, around the cross of her neck

& leans the length of our lean bed
he leans into her, we cannot look,
her shirt, open, around the cross of her neck
silver ashtray lost to the floor, no break

He leans into her, we cannot look,
unwelcome saints where girl meets spirit
silver ashtray lost to the floor, no break
feel the fire against the wood of the door

Unwelcome saints where girl meets spirit
there is no leaving now, we are here, now
feel the fire against the wood of the door
& mouth, *here, now*, over her raised back

There is no leaving now, we are here, now
the smell of metals, the beating of waists
& mouth, here, now, over her raised back
walk the length of the room to the window

The smell of metals, the beating of waists
nothing could be saved here, no, nothing
walk the length of the room to the window
greet me at my post, nothing to be salvaged

Nothing could be saved here, no, nothing
& there is no clock for yr eyes here in the room
greet me at my post, nothing to be salvaged
greet me here, push the window

& there is no clock for yr eyes here in the room
each sound is another nightmare
greet me here, push the window
wait for the tide to return

Each sound is another nightmare
she lies on his back, we turn to dress
wait for the tide to return
the elevator down is an elevator down

The white is coming from the room
she lies on his back, we turn to dress
the elevator down is an elevator down
digesting each tongue, each movement.

The Secret Annex

For Trapped Things

I.
The failed painter fires one final bullet.
The Communist and the Communist's daughters stand on our ceiling,
    sealing lips against glass.
The Harlot holds harlequin sunglasses and slides them between soft teeth.
The Light comes up, south to north, and through the window, the last bird.
Look at their breasts!
The sealed cattle car has seats of turpentine.
Beethoven lies dead in the gutter as the last canvas is set alight.
The Soldier finds the green bookcase and the silk badge: he is not hostile
    to the old leaning Lieutenant.
Songs of silken blood spiriting: storm troopers.
Look at his mouth: his nation leaping in gymnastic rings.
A list is read; two hours later a cart with their clothes is carried across.
The son, the father, the wife, each to exhaustion.
The Landing loses the loose to the water.
The Women assembling phones wrap cord, sit waiting for a letter.

II.

"Protected by a gas mask, I watched the killing myself. In the crowded cells, death came instantaneously the moment the Zyklon B was thrown in. A short, almost smothered cry, and it was all over. . . . I must even admit that this gassing set my mind at rest, for the mass extermination of the Jews was to start soon, and at that time neither Eichmann nor I was certain as to how these mass killings were to be carried out. It would be by gas, but we did not know which gas and how it was to be used. Now we had the gas, and we had established a procedure." [1]

---

1.   Rudolph Hoess' Testimony at the Post-War Nuremberg War Crime Trials.

III.

The Twins' eye color is changed and the womb removed.
The French Actress hides her FLN papers in a pocket watch.
There are weeks spent in the belly of a ship out at sea with a deck of cards
and a starched Collar.
Two Men with one triangle each are sent to the left to be deloused.
The traveling Man has no agency, sleeps with his fiddle in a curled fist
under his head.
The basements and storehouses sleep under streets of Warsaw.
In Locked Castle at No 4 Tiergartenstraße the young Boys hear Mother in
their split minds: third week, their mouths are rinds.
Catholic mother sends her Son, three weeks, a death certificate: Pneumonia.
The streets of Dazing are lined 7,000 strong, then shot, single file with
single bullet.
Four four-year-olds sit on the floor, the reports read out: a+, a+, a+, a?;
the first three enough to condemn them.
The Doctor sits down to his desk at eight in the Morning, begins printing
scrawled certificates: Typhoid, influenza, fever; by six in the
evening he puts them in the post.
Petain's Vichy fails and falls: the ship lands.

IV.

Geli Rubal took it out of the drawer for one look before putting it back to
decide. There would be four seconds pressing this to her heart, a trigger, and
then nothing. She thought herself more child than girl, going without hat
everywhere, kissing the chauffeur. She took off the gold piece from around
her heart, also her uncle's. At this remembrance she quickly took the gun
up to her chest, leveled it, and closed her eyes. Four seconds. Trigger.

V.

The Thirteen Principles of Faith

1. *I believe with complete faith that the Creator, Blessed is His Name, creates and guides all creatures and that He alone, made, makes, and will make everything.*
2. *I believe with complete faith that the Creator, Blessed is His Name, is unique, and there is no uniqueness like His in any way, and that He alone is our God, Who was, Who is, and Who always will be.*
3. *I believe with complete faith that the Creator, Blessed is His Name, is not physical and is not affected by physical phenomena, and that there is no comparison whatsoever to Him.*
4. *I believe with complete faith that the Creator, Blessed is His Name, is the very first and the very last.*
5. *I believe with complete faith that the Creator, Blessed is his name— to Him alone is it proper to pray and it is not proper to pray to any other.*
6. *I believe with complete faith that all the words of the prophets are true.*
7. *I believe with complete faith that the prophecy of Moses our teacher, peace upon him, was true, and that he was the father of the prophets— both those who preceded him and those who followed him.*
8. *I believe with complete faith that the entire Torah now in our hands is the same one that was given to Moses, our teacher, peace be upon him.*
9. *I believe with complete faith that this Torah will not be exchanged nor will there be another Torah from the Creator, Blessed is His Name.*
10. *I believe with complete faith that the Creator, Blessed is His Name, knows all the deeds of human beings and their thoughts, as it is said, 'He fashions their hearts all together, He comprehends all their deeds.'*
11. *I believe with complete faith that the Creator, Blessed is His Name, rewards with good those who observe His commandments, and punishes those who violate His commandments.*

12. *I believe with complete faith in the coming of the Messiah, and that he will come.*
13. *I believe with complete faith that there will be a resuscitation of the dead whenever the wish emanates from the Creator, Blessed is His Name and exalted is His mention, forever and for all eternity.*

For Your salvation I do long, Hashem.
I do long, Hashem for Your salvation.
Hashem, for Your salvation I do long.

VI.

"There were, however, individual cases where my men were shocked by the inhumanity of the Hungarian police. It was reported to me that the Hungarians were driving the Jews into the cars like cattle to a slaughterhouse. It sometimes happened that there were too few slop buckets on the trains, too little drinking water or no drinking water at all, or that the provisions were bad or stolen during the loading. Cars were overloaded to empty the debarkation camp as quickly as possible. You can imagine how it was when the Hungarians ordered, 'everybody in, in, in. The border comes in 240 kilometers, and then Germany. Let the Germans finish things up.' Several times I reminded the Hungarian government in writing—nothing was done orally in my office—that we did not want to punish individual Jews. We wanted a political solution. Even our own units were guilty of roughness here and there. I once saw a soldier beat a frail old Jew over the head with a rubber club. I spoke to the soldier, reported him to his commander and demanded he be punished and demoted. Himmler would not stand for that kind of thing. That is sadism." [2]

VII.

Girls in their school uniform: skirts and blouses and army boots.
Five students drop white paper down long staircases: hung by ears hour later.

---

2.   Adolph Eichmann, Adolph Eichmann Trial.

Millions of fresh-faced youth raise an arm; hundreds twist in caverns.

The Doctor has his license revoked, his practice stripped.

Churches fill with Wagner as the chorus is interrupted by shouts.

The old woman is peddling flowers on the street when the first pane is punched in.

Over dinner, mein Führer likes to talk about dog breeding, Darwin, and the process by which lipstick is made from goose fat.

The boy boards a plane heading east eight hours, kisses mother goodbye.

The Marxist sits holding his head behind the paper hoping to be passed over in the square.

The hospital workers inflate patients who are torn from their systems come nightfall.

VIII.

Yizkor

> *Hashem, what is man that You recognize him? The son of a frail human that You reckon with him?*
>
> *Man is like a breath, his days are passing shadows.*
>
> *In the morning it blossoms and is rejuvenated, by evening it is cut down and brittle.*
>
> *According to the count of our days, so many, You teach us; Then we shall acquire a heart of wisdom.*
>
> *Safeguard the perfect and watch the upright, for the destiny of that man is peace.*
>
> *But God will redeem my soul from the grip of the Lower World, For He will take me, Selah!*
>
> *My flesh and my heart yearn— Rock of my heart, and my portion is God, forever.*
>
> *Thus the dust returns to the ground as it was, and the spirit returns to God who gave it.*

for one's mother

May God remember the soul of my Mother, my teacher, who has gone on to her world, because, without making a vow, I shall give to charity on her behalf. As reward for this, may her soul be bound in the Bond of Life, together with the souls of Abraham, Isaac, and Jacob; Sarah, Rebecca, Rachel, and Leah; and together with the other righteous men and women in the Garden of Eden. Now let us respond: Amen.

for martyrs

O God, full of mercy, Who dwells on high, grant proper rest on the wings of the Divine Presence—in the lofty levels of the holy and the pure ones, who shine like the glow of the firmament— for the souls of (all my relatives, both on my father's side and on my mother's side), the holy and pure ones who were killed, murdered, slaughtered, burned, drowned and strangled for the sanctification of the Name, (through the hands of the German oppressors, may their name and memory be obliterated) because, without making a vow, I will contribute to charity in remembrance of their souls. May their resting place be in the Garden of Eden—Therefore may the Master of mercy shelter them in the shelter of His wings for eternity; and may He bind their souls in the Bond of Life. Hashem is their heritage, and may they repose in peace on their resting places. Now let us respond: Amen.

IX.

Sophie is the one on the left with the White Rose.
Hans is her brother, next to her, holding the papers.
Christoph holds the match.
Kurt is the older man, back blocking the light.
Alex and Willi, right and further right, in uniform.

The men had just returned from the front—
Deployed on academic holiday.

Hans kisses his sister on the neck.

X.

Margo is taken; her body still warm when I go, too.
Lethe is a place we spend the rest of our lives, bloated, belly up, floating.
Otto cannot even cry now; the glucose from the factory in his tear ducts.
In the fallout shelter, the baby is slapped to cry and then removed.
His grandmother sent to die and he, refused by the academy.
The boy stands in the Beer Hall Putsch, a Moses, the people parting.
The boy stands head down, feet bare.
The boy bevels the edges of one nation in one world.
Gates to hell: all shoulders against the door.
Three cigarettes shaken out of the pack, three privates pause.
The young girl tugs at her mother's hand, leads her up the stairs.
This is Valhalla.
The Globe is drawn: women, you insects, bare the babe.

XI.

Sodom by the Sea

He slid his thumbs into my eye sockets and pressed.
That was the way he killed me.

It was 1920 again,
You could tell by the way he sat in his car,
All white behind this beach color on his face,
Confused by it and warmed by its leather and pleased.

He looked over at me, lying, pleased
That I was on this beach but not that I was there, pressed
For time and knowing the turned smile on his face—
And I looked at him thinking this will be how, near his car,
And looking at him, knowing him, knowing me,

This will be how we leave again,
It will be back to the various forms of veto again,
And I knew that this would not be amusing, nor would I be pleased.
Knowing him knowing me—

Knowing this, I gathered my skirt and went to wait in the car
He, seeing this, got out of it, and started smoking, pressing
The butt of the rolled cigarette: the beach meanwhile blinding
against his face—

This is how I noticed me, and my face in his face
This was where I said, again,

I would leave: pressing out all thought of the beach, pressing
Out all thoughts of all faces, all thoughts that pleased
Pressing the tight leather of the car,
Of the car seat, I held fast to it, waiting, while he held fast to me.

Later, many months after ours, Edison died, and after me,
He sat along the water, on the dock with a long face
Where mine had been, and again
He smoked, and in a new car—

And the scene, totally rearranged, was much the same, for he was pleased.
Her body near bare, and her shoulders, which he was pressing
Went pale at his touch and her color rose under the weight of the press
And he undressed himself, and I could not look far off, knowing me,
Not modest. And all could see his pleasure
And her white shoulders moving near his face.

He looked at me, knowing I was seated under my skirts on the hood
        of the car.
And they sat there day after day again and again.
And the wind blew me around, and his eyes darkened in his face as I left,
Pressed along in the air, his pleasure fading. The car skirted the road
        against the high
Cliffs, and again and again the pale woman said, marvelous,
        marvelous, grand day, yes.

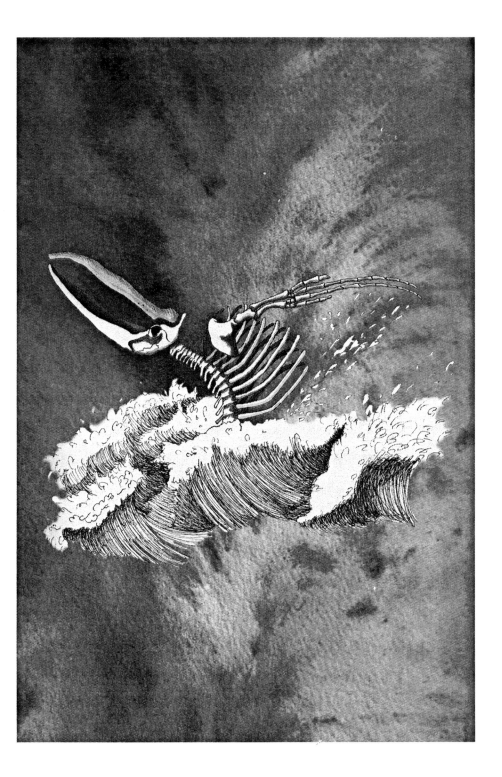